THE SEA IN-BETWEEN

Dianne Cikusa

Copyright © 2018 Dianne Cikusa

All rights reserved

The moral right of the author has been asserted in accordance with the Copyright Amendment (Moral Rights) Act 2000.

All rights reserved. Except as permitted under the Australian Copyright Act 1968 (for example, fair dealing for the purposes of study, research, criticism or review) no part of this publication may be reproduced, stored in a retrieval system, or transmitted in any form or by any means, electronic, mechanical, photocopying, recording or otherwise, without the written permission of the publisher.

Cataloguing-in-Publication entry is available from the National Library of Australia: http://catalogue.nla.gov.au/

National Library of Australia Cataloguing-in-Publication:

Author: Cikusa, Dianne (1973–)

Title: The Sea In-Between

ISBN: 978-0-9943257-6-1

Subjects: Poetry

Photographer: Cikusa, Dianne

Front cover image and internal drawings licensed from AdobeStock

Internal photographs © Dianne Cikusa

Back cover image © Dianne Cikusa

Published by Mignon Press, 2018
PO Box 922, Katoomba NSW 2780

mignon
PRESS

Also by Dianne Cikusa:

Hope and Substance

Death's brother, Sleep.

Virgil

CONTENTS

THE MATADOR: FLAWS OF MOTION 1
    AMBITION 4
    DEDICATIONS 6
    CHOOK RAFFLE 8
    PRIVATE READING 10
    SINNER'S CHILD 12
    INDIGENOUS 14
    TEMPERANCE 16
    PARRICIDE 18
    MANNEQUIN 20
    LETTERS TO EDITOR 22
    RAUCOUS VENDORS 24
    GREEK WEDDING 26
    CHARLATAN 28
    NEW YORKER 30
    CORNERED HUMOUR 32
    SYMMETRY 34
    PRIMITIVE SCRIPT 36
    EMERGENCE 38
    INCANTATION 40
    BLEACHED BIRDS 42
    HARDENED CANDY 44
    CHEAP SOUVENIRS 46

CONVERSION FACTOR	48
ROUTINE FREIGHT	50
EXHIBITION	52
GRANITE KITCHEN	54
JAMMED TRANSLATION	56
PEREGRINATION	58
EINSTEIN'S ABACUS	60
LOSING STREAK	62
PARTISANS	64
AN EYELID ON FAMILY	66
IMPOTENT WIGS	68
SILENCE	70
UNWRITTEN ARTICLE	72
THE LAST TOY SOLD	74

CHINESE WHISPERS: POEMS IN TRANSIT ... 77

MOVING STATUE	80
SCENARIOS	82
JAMAICAN GENTLEMAN	84
JUNCTION	86
AKASHA	88
TREE–FELLER	90
SYMPATHY BOAT	92
EXCAVATION	94
NEXUS	96
GUSHING FOUNTAIN	98
NUMBERLESS	100

SAGE	102
MEMORABILIA	104
SIENNA	106
FATHER	108
GUARDIAN	110
IRON ORE	112
NARCISSUS	114
EMPORIUM	116
TRANSLUCENT PROMISE	118
DOGFIGHT	120
HAIRPIN	122
CONVERGING TRIBES	124
SLANT STRIDES	126
HEXAGON	128
OWNERS OF PROCESS	130
RELAPSES	132
KHAKI	134
BLACKOUT	136
MY CONDOLENCES	138
MANDALA	140
LEATHER FORMATIONS	142
HOVERING PANIC	144
ORANGE EXPLOSIVES	146
FOUNTAIN PEN	148
EXTRACTION	150
UNSOLICITED	152

RED AND PINK SONGBOOKS: WASHED POETICS...... 155

    THE SEA IS FOR SALE 158

    FUTILE SCISSORS 160

    IVORY BURROW 162

    DAYLIGHT 164

    AMPERSAND 166

    SOFTENED SKETCH 168

    ALTRUISTIC CROISSANT 170

    PATRIOT LOVER 172

    GEOMETRY 174

    HAIKU 176

    HITCHHIKER 178

    ISTHMUS 180

    SALT CRYSTALS 182

    RED SKIES 184

    SITAR 186

    PSYCHIC TRILOGY 188

    DEPARTING 190

    PRAISE 192

    THE BLUE ROOM 194

    O-ZONE 196

    SYLLABUS 198

    ALCHEMIST 200

    SNOWMAKER 202

    AMPHIBIANS 204

    PARANORMAL 206

CINNAMON EYES 208
OVA 210
AMETHYST 212
THE CHRISTENING 214
RETROGRADE 216
AUBERGINE MOON 218
SABBATICAL QUEEN 220
SAFFRON TRAIN 222
THE SETTLEMENT 224
ENDING SONG 226
THE ARTIST THAT DID MAUVE 228

Acknowledgements: 233
About the author: 235
About this book: 237

THE MATADOR:
FLAWS OF MOTION

AMBITION

Breathe yourself
out of the picture,
there's no rapid escape path

(-- butterfly is pinned down)

They've taken progress
for granted,
leaving behind their
saviour at the altar;
Wads
of marriage certificates
bound by elastic bands

Wading through complex
proxy:
unauthorised swimmers
caught in driftnets,
perceiving through
large holes (that
biggest words only can
fall through),
  as if they were
educated
in sonar language)))))))

The ergonomics of
modern number-crunching:

…you thought you were
earning employment…
sadly,
the meltdown of tears
left us smeared in biblical grief

Heart-racing achievement
is no longer in vogue,
and looking
yet for mogul equivalent

man's world is
seeking
the perfect microclimate.

DEDICATIONS

did you speculate a life?
Or an immortal living?

Prologue
is laughing hard—

stupid pages, who
won't let me look
inside,
that I may recall
the volume of substance for them

recording readers
abusers
& rudely-related incidents

Accidental blurb
about to spill
onto the next pecking level

(I'm packing the avalanche
before it happens)
sobriety
has marked on my calendar

Dear God, this
thirteenth day of December
our dictators and neighbours

are strutting cross-country
    (remember—
draping tinsel

you pulled it down
from the window)

Gold clasp [second notch]
( ) a designated logo
  &
sketchy introduction:
   [: even as we understand the
buffer of pretentious dreams]:
so too, Remember—the chiselled tree
with fastened leaf,
the din engulfed by padlock.

CHOOK RAFFLE

This is
your lucky day

No. 19
could generously feed
the entire population

Teach and
correspond:
we need a mother
who will
whisk—not beat
the egg

One-hundred-and-one methods
to fry bread crumbs
wingless
skinless
Boneless

[chickens without a crutch]

make a wish
Blow out happy birthday / and
    grant us single serve proportion

A different type
of door

leads out
to the hatchery
[···time your entry into the barrel]

There's no one here
but a prize drawer,
Golden winner
(tap him on the head)
if ready,
Place shell
gently on unscratched
surface—
allow to simmer for 3 soft minutes
He will boil the instant
he realises he has become dinner.

PRIVATE READING

cruel fate,
Who asked that you come along?

[bring in the recitalist of luck]
impetus wears a sceptical label
 and turns out
uncomplimentary autograph;

Decorum fostered
authentically in glass jars:
a hydroponic ripening
 docile faces
in the cool room
and pallid corpses requiring lift

Sirens
and crawling paramedics
Awakened, they run
with sturdy urgency;
we marvel
again at
what is haughtily treasured;

desecrated tidbits
Tattered abductions
of aspiration—his, not hers

She is medium-rare lady,

grooming
 a dominant hairdo
Forkful of curls
that he tunnels into his mouth

   [- insignificant complaint -]
lightning bolt is tucked away
Behind a brittle ear.

SINNER'S CHILD

I've got
plenty of guilt to spare,

leftover
from the scraps of
mother's birth

cordless
phone lines:
we receive disdain in moderation
  Miss with flavoured contempt,
your scorn outweighs us all;

how pained and righteous are we,
munificently exhorting the Sacred

Placenta
is worth the attachment of
half-a-kilogram,
as it provides ample examination
of what's in the forager's basket

make illicit offering
and promise
that the bluest sky
will not secretly swindle
(liar—
see, it's raining)

reconstruct
the spaciousness of
warmth
woman cried and bled
Father tried, and said:
'Where am I still lost from home?'

You've left a scar
Mummy,
since my bellybutton always feels empty

[I'm missing you]
and Lord, I hate to miss the program
in favour of commercial.

INDIGENOUS

cobalt executives
bidding
on a sun-baked academy,
Liberty lost
in aquamarine slabs

invested motifs
stuck to violet crêpe paper

bespoken tea cosy
won't give way
to non-authentic inheritances
I've only my guardian
and cast-iron setbacks

rummaging through satellites
and ticking meteors
Hire a new cast at
half-price, [not at all
unlike the glib
and suave director]
lazy technician
flicks the switch on a new landscape
Refreshed,
awoken spuriously blessed

Stationed at the influential point
of laser beams

Hold—
veneration
Wrestling with reverence is an
earnest challenge
Pale saint is waiting at the juncture,
closing in around steep ridges
and paint-spattered mountains

splashing of bill posters
catches the eyes too soon

deafening advertisements: did we miss the
brooding figure, in support of
 a princely event?
splitting hairs
of prima donnas
She will flit among prissy domain.

TEMPERANCE

Blow my trumpet
Thy cradle has seen fit
to clasp reticent finger
around air of simplest minds
{--} inside the confines
 of
 bought tranquillity

Nights' tendrils
and maiden's symphonic lullaby
gave breath the quiet meaning
she so ardently sought
to transpose
And inversely compose
by the white mirror
of his lucid comprehension
(a sombre expanse:)

No provision affixes
to the glares made by unfair dismissal
of ominous hearts,
 where prosperity
was the only blatant cause of concern

hushed alcove
is tugging
at a baleful continent
Imperial charm, [the aura

of a bleached sunset]

billowing winds
and effusive tribulation;
our troubles propped easily
upon elbows that caress
Hope
with cartoon momentum

like uninterrupted flames⋯

Lewd demand is perched haggardly
upon fingers of gnarled courtesy
bulk—
is constructed
with sprawling satisfaction.

PARRICIDE

It is up to oneself to
peruse the directory,
as there is seldom
any typical explanation ~

Fancy how we tickle
interpretation
And whet
one another's appetite ~~ ~~

God is falsely claimed
No left turn,
but U-turns are
permitted, once you've
reached the
flameproof gateway

(ninety-nine) is also
c/- number 9
can we subsist on
in-house movies
 and provisional humour?
stroked allusion
[for the greased cynic]

Somnolent ushers in a
dank and dirty cinema
could inadvertently tell

that *We All* left our shoes
on the floor, before
walking out
on our partner
during X-rated crimes
[Save for a sunny outlook
made ready amid friends]
Viewfinders welded shut
    until jolted opening
Those lurid appurtenances
were eye-catching,
rather like throwaway cups
& popcorn confetti
Can-opener for a
trashy tossing of exploits

* mystique guaranteed

Mistrust is commonplace
in balmy atmospheres.

MANNEQUIN

dishevelled supermodel
 and a
badly-designed human
 Two heads,
coLLide within a single face :-:

Behind-the-scenes hooks
spur on the shows
of merchandising
amongst fraternising peddler

Identical coffee-maker
unidentified laughter;
dummy body [with
store-bought remote]; /Control

tied her wrists
with sequins
(then slashed them)
hysteria
of magnetic bondage
shop owner hoots
(this is on-the-job lechery)

Sales hit good target, shoppers
loving to lay under more concrete

black beetle

   and a
red-and-green ladybird
Sorry, but we do *not* compensate
  on colour, (&
      for
  exchange, you must stock
extra proof of identity)
Thanks again for the lovely array
  of once-worn items

we sewed them onto fireworks
then passed the buck.

LETTERS TO EDITOR

leaden silhouettes
impel towards
an effigy built into the wall,
 behind sneering picture frames

my only prop
 is
the shadow of Hir own soul,
projecting
inside a provocative room

Tried
to re-spell your name,
but my eraser just won't work

Intimacy
is beyond the scope of this article,
 enclosed
you will only find the story of
an explorer who lost his bearings

pity those whose grated
hooves
the media watched,
whilst combing through personal files
The brush off—
glamour's taken yet another turn

Could we provide a water bottle
for the camel? she's
inundated
by the backlog of journalism
[Please re-address the mail you
scrawled on the coveted bellies
of middle-eastern harlots]
nicknamed convenors mustered up a
non-committal scribe whose writing's
been
refunded…(*shush*, I do not wish to usher
the opportunist into my lounge room)
likely counterplot and defeated golfers

Conservatoriums
opened sliding doors.

RAUCOUS VENDORS

The recommended retail is
serving up a garbled price,

take-away
the roadblock; fast-food
makes for quicker servitude

[consult
 the pre-paid calendar]
Dial in with
childlike inquisition
and demand liberal postage

 until the latter caves in

[unswerving deliverance]:
Apology is stumbling
to forget the last line;
check out to whom ingratitude
made out the final sentence
(then cash in your code name)

Cut from the squad—
only a patch
of white-chalked numbers anyway

Move on as vagabond will,
dealing refuge in siesta:

we among the sleeping brotherhood
are blending interwoven dreams
 [: a hypermarket]
bliss
travels the longest road
 Utopia is a rocky street
(wheeling along) four-lane freeways

reputedly,

they left room for a parked bus
 and a pram in transit.

GREEK WEDDING

Smashed platelets,
 another
broken crockpot
        (: & dizzy head):   :
we're scrubbing you out from
 our unblemished list
of orthodox principles
 [we won't
accept you in this cul-de-sac]

Films, movies (and surnames)
are unwinding,
Our fair dinkum photographer
takes
post-dated pictures—
besides his first backdated one

thickest
slice of cake; rhapsody of crumbs
Largest tumbler of wine
and guests inebriated
beyond distinction
All accents mixed into the punch
  (···rope in next doors' bitter fruit-flavour)
We leave in dour spirits,
sunrise
is overwhelmed
by yesterday's revelry

[: a fast and furious honeymoon]

female pistil
he's prising open the
flower tonight
Sickened by the
sense
of religious excuse; fervour
should not have leaned
so far over the picket fence

Olives, cheese
and a singed pasta sauce,
fights with

 meagre serving of wild rice.

CHARLATAN

We never draw to a close
what has been dispelled
with rudimentary flippancy,

rotund emotion:)
I am shouting
at God's gift-wrapping efforts
and His indirect evaluation,
 [we tied
the best knots too late]

>>> *a lurching heart*
  is openly perplexed

Why is my menacing grip
gravely clad
in the whiff of repulsion?

Calmly, I squiggle emotional
blackmail
into the web of forefingers,
an effective tactic
to apprehend the rival
(who won't stop nattering)

[Oblique interrogation]: / take a stab
at opaque affiliation
Should I gently throw them off

the summit
of their venturous decision? ¿

befuddled turnaround; blunt mask
has negotiable talk-time
and cantilevered resolve
Like clockwork,
they console the other party
on the boughs of drooping branches,
swathed in solid colour
 and cooling complexion
[baffled hagglers]
interceding at long-last
(particularity leading to culverts of desire)
Masochism: the state of mind
we often find meandering.

NEW YORKER

Rats from big-city trenches

dumped shares in
poverty's lap—
What didn't belong to them
was begging for demerits
 (/briefly,
The Suit explains himself)

their patois
 makes a ribbed guess, while he
adds up shifting tensions

the Art world is suggestive:
Sharpened pencils
live here too, you know—
snapped chalk
jots down latest index,
and consumer prices goods
according to -/ the permeable demand

Emotional gastritis sank his teeth
deep in the washbowls of jargon,
then went off
to market a new brand of diaper

arborist tied up the gamesman
and banker [such an

exquisite piece of work]

coal-black workers
cleaned up remaining debris, And built
more jungles
of concrete rebellion;
grubbiest fingers
clung to frenetic tracks
⋯linking forgotten personages
whose memberships had expired
That we so quickly lost our home; Sulking
Timetable—got run over;
Agonies too tired, to tell the cab driver
when to stop driving over puddles.

CORNERED HUMOUR

Did you notice
the lights
were home,
  but the grown-ups
were out ? ?

Threading objectives
      through the eye
  of an
 antiquated keyhole…

have they unfinished business?
or are they just suited
to the soundtrack
of their self-neglect?

meanwhile, meticulous envy
is propped against
the broom cupboard
Waiting for
opportunities to build
a makeshift teepee,
[unimpeachably] off-limits

and secured
    in unequivocal hectares

  Seriously—

was it just an accident?
Or did they really mean
to be so faithfully horrid,
The torrent
of five-star demand
being so-so overwhelming

champagne barricades
 For those gaping feelings
we found unfashionable

Protection is safe—
but not always biodegradable.

SYMMETRY

These
  jolly introductions
are decoding by duration:
     May we
  proofread
biased captions?

When one is counting
looms of speech,
The water has already begun its
imagined journey - - *Can't you see?* - -

backwards
 slips not into a marginal past,
but into twilight
 (and we never honestly
moved forward)

From the rear, one can never spot
one's rowdy resemblance;
Culpability
astutely reminds the drunkard
    (from the farthest gutter:)   -||-
They took my child
 she was yelping inside,
Tied down
 by anonymous seatbelt to
convivial charades

and cherished narcissism;

pretence leans on the arm of parody,
then wisdom casts a grand shadow
I can (just) hear
The vapours of my old life;
Once birthed a fellow who rolled
around in a cigar⋯pleading that⋯
he couldn't stop paddling in rubble

Or fossicking for grain—
   the seed bed rising above mounds
where we'd buried musk-scented pellets

With the crowd in a heap,
it was easy to pick up
the clippings of informal ordeal.

PRIMITIVE SCRIPT

[splendiferous] embraces
broke apart
   in- the- nick- of time;

flaccid lungs
 squelched out of place,
creativity clogged
in a choking throat

invisible lodgings / masking
 the Flecks of reassembled verdict;
the rolling drunks
were clearly disqualified
(and so-say all of us)

erecting totem poles
    {feather in the rain,
       father in the ground}
pooling implicit wisdom···
Broadcasting the eclipse

a vespertine outburst:
night-time got flattened

- - - - - - - only an adversary
was holed up in self-sufficing
residence, where somebody's
composition had won a foul prize

stilettos
cemented in the traffic, shoelaces
strapped to the roundabout

Hailstorms
pelted animals—we
cried again, They
died again
smear the donkey
scribbled elephants
(maltreated behind fence)

serving spoon
rushes to greet the dinner plates.

EMERGENCE

He who loves me
must govern
beneath
a venial umbrella--
      Give & Take:
for man, money/
(the rooted evil)
for woman, sex and
bumptious request

amorous stop-watch
And
eager bracelets

man thinks
he is Stud
(she drops her earrings,
then cries)

diamantes smashed
by strongest effort
The abacus lost count
in broken beads of sweat

pondering devastation:
hedonism
is embedded in the veins
[- inspect my collection

of prattling obsessions-]

labyrinth
of tyranny:
Silly kitten
  atop a leaning precipice,
lapping after blood at
horror's pointed hedges

[The ladled integrity
has flavourless taste]

I have niggling feeling that
I'm not the only anchored
Prisoner

INCANTATION

'Talk quietly, please!!!'
said the
last vegetable on earth

revolution is prejudiced

[: raptorial snakes
trailing after
vibrating melody]

tectonic umpire
seismic punters
 [magnified in moonlight]
Her
field is widely open - - - -
 last year,
they
scolded the starfish
for lavish commodity
 while he
drank copious oxygen
and extended narration

(via a boastful radius)

Teams made best pledge
to commemorate only
the captain;

Others were always
jostling and scaremongering
for compliance by means
 of a convertible symbol—
   Allocated parameters:
walk back five paces
and stand in your memories

[drop down] lawless ornament
frontrunner will snigger
at cardboard leaflet
before escaping into
            hinterland.

BLEACHED BIRDS

Talons connecting to
the universal branch,
　...awaiting generic trial
　[virtuous tails
are scarce, we see]

cardboard television (that
Box with Cut-out Hole)
forms malefic opinion
and looks for ideal vantage points

Do not disturb all those
narrow eyelets encased
in sweaty body bags,
　nor all the beer swilling men
in public bar, selling animal crowd

[Ornithologist found
　better prey to do :]

heinous turbines
propel an outback generator;
Σ Only the bloke clothed in revenue
sustains an unspoiled feeling- Σ - Σ

don't blow off hydroelectricity
'cause of embittered posture;
new-fangled additions

escalate to an already overgrown
population (reaping hisses
of familial emotion)

caution is emphatically withdrawn
Dismissals are common
silken missiles
exiled patrons
Puffing chests: What kind of man
Spills ashtrays in the basement?

HARDENED CANDY

sugar-coated cubes
  screwed the lid off each
and every round jar—

unreservedly, they filled
their stomachs
with helpings of berries
and wild mushrooms
Scented classrooms
guided children
down plotting roads

 and scheming tangents,
Swarthy avenues lined
by windswept manors
and unrestricted airflows
[belching
homogenous ownership]

Cul-de-sacs
of fuming proprietors and
lost property, leased out
 to elapsed maiden names
and mis-represented Sirs

Ageing authors bit down
on the dust of their crusty lives
and mouldy attitudes

Fungal sores looked worse
under the light of budding truth
Yet no one near
saw fit to discuss what was of
strategic relevance,
for want of declining income
and reclining self-importance

Retroactive skin-care
nourishing the repair of intellect:
The youthful quotient
raised by hydraulic leverage

Please thank
all those old endorsements.

CHEAP SOUVENIRS

life, is incontestably
 ripping us off
at the busiest corner

buy a ticket (---one-way---------->)
escorting into a timeless map

depreciated craftsmen:
 obliterated lines
 on
colossal traders' stand

Girlie magazines are a
good read, but of
poorest taste, like rabid comics

bulldozed newsprint
put every reader behind bars—
tables,
graphs and pie chart
acknowledged yesteryear's
sales figures

Third-world market-seller
makes
his barest living from
hawking at the periphery

mainstream woman
is alive, but lacks
means of overt support
So then, is God testing us
through our desperation,
　His non-intervention
and unrelenting shores;

We believed
in the feats
of those who scampered across
into alien rabbit farms,
carrying a torch of trapped inner hope
They won't share the flurry of anonymity,
　Lethal doses, now plunging new hazard
into the windshield.

CONVERSION FACTOR

an Insider. Listening skills
multiplied—devised mazes
and crosswords
A couple of puzzled faces

an Outsider. The clapping
is incessant; invoked
wrath is sublime
        and faceless [ ]

the Educationalist is rightly
snubbed, where students
are concerned
Chairperson nudges himself
 constructively
into the twenty-first century

expediently applied material;
adhesives think out loud, so that
the collage
can be arranged decoratively

and that
···makes three thoughts
worth writing
down [next to aborted sums]

Why they didn't hear

why I was
complaining, was
presumably an elemental error

Had we not encountered traces
of denigration, our own self
would have wildly insinuated
that
we had trodden the museum wall
in bare feet: [virtual gallery]:
A lozenge for the mind
(Plus a teaspoonful
of twinkling flirtation)

Venturing dynamo
converged the lecturer's galaxy.

ROUTINE FREIGHT

Their designated train
is making its
thunderous point—
 exclamation hurtles
from an itemised list- -- --

Panic button
 [pressed] fast-forward

Wise cattle
eat the thinnest
blades of grass,
 and graze
after the rest of the herd
(they're deaf,
these big eyes)

don't they hear the sound
of their own terror?
it's coming up to tell you
that you've come here to die...

chew your cud
and go home;
 mist
is quietly peering through the fences,
 unfazed by a
doubtless oversupply of aphorisms

Electrical charge delivers
jolt to the calf
Watch your step on tilted ground
[shadows are reviving]
with racked nerves upon seaboard
 (-you look good crouching
on a foam tray-)

Expert grocer
Export game player.

EXHIBITION

Historical theatre (had__curtly undraped
innumerable performers   );   ____and the
chronological actors were crestfallen__

then⋯ [a scene set on fish street]:
Oil streaks
were chartered
to sail across the swimmers'
pain,
with plinth slipping

　　　[Bogus voyage
of debilitated links]

Do a doublethink: Somebody
who will deliberate
the shadowed end of the world

twenty-one persons
evacuating:
Fire supply is

{ quivering }

with sentimentality,
Storybooks rising from the sewer

a demoralising curator

reads out
from his pompous microphone,
   and henceforth starts philandering

On stand-by, are scratched statues
with chipped noses [and stung rationale]

The presiding influence remains unmoved
by iconoclast; with Institutes lacking features,
that we could easily pass on
the spool of proper ideas

Afterwards, untangle the
graphic inventory
and mourn the fading daylight.

GRANITE KITCHEN

<< I have sold the price
 of pain >>
Interesting, they said,
before they siphoned
the last strangled breath
from my dying alveoli

We care *not*,
that you live or die
Suicide is fun to watch,
because it's *you*, you see
not me, nor I, nor we

babies are born
(if-only) to cry each day
This journey—
may drag just
one ambassador at a time

hooray, it's gut-wrenching
stuff, so wonderfully volatile,

 coaxing the spirit's ingenuity

But (always a but)
we *still* don't care
It's not happening to *us*

We've pasted shut our
eyelids,
such plastered views of defiance;
He is drunk on his foe
She is guarding her malevolent
temper

lettering underpinned
to
the jacket that wipes its sleeve
on my chin;
perpetual hypertension
 Erupting anxiety
Goddess
is becoming quite vocal in the dark.

JAMMED TRANSLATION

Definitive words ain't
moving anywhere—

conversely, tentative lingo
blesses the foreigner,
so long as indifference
is not wedged in between

Conspired breath: validated
minutes tick over
like volcanic time-bombs,
 thirst never fed quantities
of
starved flames

womb
 like a gorge; empty
Fathomless
never savoured, rudely conserved
headstrong accents;
idioms
bent and mangled
The universe
is tricking every presumption,
        memory-joggers
            waiting for autocues

Enough-- is never enough--

and idleness
finds no viscous relief
Calamity strikes by the hands
of twelve o'clock
Is effluence the problem
of environmentalists?
Or bronzed politicians,
whose every mouthful
leads through to a perfunctory den
  of rote-learned excuse
and begrudging discovery;

we welcome details on
debilitated mammals
      (monitor REM pattern)

Seek lost-and-found
in my new-age dictionary.

PEREGRINATION

his domineering
wing

spans
the distance of Heaven's heart

Spokesman said that
flighty wanderings
were the stalker's nightmare

for he couldn't catch
the vulture
of his own shadow…

splinters—
would take on mammoth proportions,
the size of a naked eye
Perhaps a disused claw
 or shirking foot;
The chicken might
have better chance

Of escaping unscathed
if her feathers
would sooner roost,
Than roast

Falcon, Eagle—(& an almighty

sparrow)
soaring
over common prey
Rendering the helpless mortal
as sidekick
to cumulative whim

cloudless response to craving;
Man-made machinery
no longer has simple impact.

EINSTEIN'S ABACUS

Lion-tamer stopped
counting down
the days to opening night
      [: premier pupils
  have decisive eyes
on the curtain]

Ten...
nine...
eight...
unfledged builders
resprayed the
wooden chair; Beech grain
 and a
brightly painted stool;
 nursery colours
played with notorious swirls
for an admonishing effect;

Cobras rising (furtively)
to the façades
of peeled history,
Turbans moulding around
thick foreheads
of unbending culture and
stooping shoulder blades;
Java's emperor
sporting the blood

of spilled covenant

[drafted armies:] tear-jerkers
filing in succession the
barbarity, botched wizardry
 and physiognomy of jezebels

Asian fast-food
declares independent warfare
on
local food chain;
 buy-back crumpled wrappers

Sauté in globs
 of abstemious virility
and swooning hippies.

LOSING STREAK

Quarantine of early
ideas:]
sardonic diaries

and impious
saliva forming at the
sides of the mouth
 [determination
quashed
by the mercenary presence
of others] ~
well-wishers
Injecting a subtle decree
for materialistic losses

roulette wheel
of odds and ends,
tax brackets
 and tetchy misfortunes

Or missed fortunes,
dearest décor takes
fragrant strolls through a monastery

Have we scattered tufts
in the closet, and bred
flea-ridden toupee?
anticipated prototypes might

in that case fly away

The predictable glue
has now dried out
Re-application required
(but no refs essential)

that anyone may gamble
That everybody will lose,
[shouldn't we?] take part
in this pandemic tomfoolery—

solid temperament will not rest
in mortal portfolio.

PARTISANS

devotees
of commercialism
···are commenting on deficits

young feelings
are nothing
but inflammatory judgements
smothered pink,
dipped in
lemon-flavoured smiles
and cordoned off
from the general public

[# shut up in ordinal cages #]

Sub-divisions are
marked in my almanac,
with partial dates highlighted

the profit margins
between countries
and customs
are floundering—
non-supportive and spineless

it's first-class deflection,
however the
repercussions are endless;

The trinity of brothers
is broken
by rough handling

faithfully,
 we envied you
!-- never mind the telecast was
swivelling to meet up
with generations of mundane
convention-- [greet the banal joker]

Shrug off
the pock-marked accord,
It is altogether just a gratified hum.

AN EYELID ON FAMILY

The celestial war of races
has instigated
yellow zones of purgatory—
Salvation is arranged in themes
And so without ado,
we're
    playing back the
songs of our inexperience;

empirical research
observed [better and best]
 the discrepancy
in multi-layered archives

Town planner announces
the blueprint for next grid,
inclusive of graduations
&
 driving interdependence

Climbing steep fences,
 we survey a
detracting medley:
nothing sparks recent interest
in this cultural battlefield
Today rather lacks excitement
(except for the meat-worker)

improvised languages
 and
reproved networks
(mind-your-own-business)

Freelancing critiques
brought together
isolated stimulation; lacerated
expansion of destitute offenders
Slamming doors
Only plant pot flourishes.

IMPOTENT WIGS

fallacy
 stands in the roomiest
apartment,
apprising one's troubled self

[acrostic abode]
The initial assertion—is
an emollient
to posterior friction

(gee, how we love to
dangle
 the fishing line of
reaction,

Since your door
is always open)

let us in
(*.#! damn this) busted latch
heroines need their space too

lubricant says yes:
 'tis a seasonal joke between
bartender & bodhisattva

    glittering headdresses
  blazing through

monotones of sheer boredom
The crime of sunlight…

post-modern ink
//two-tone weaving/

Then came the post-mortem:
) she drowned in the cacophony
of egoistic babble(((
Cascading consonants without
shutter speed
to arrest nude image;
imploding anguish has been shipped
to dry location

[Rest in piece]

SILENCE

#Click: [and—here—we—are]
campaigning
  for collective restoration
of antiques & auxiliary bargains

Likewise,
are purveyors on standby—
shabbily clad,
adhering to bare-limbed alteration

escalating cynicism
in erudite context; who of whom
 is educating?
placid alien, play-acting human

}. }. }. the skill of
grasshoppers
numbing the mind by night,
separating the process
of intermingling attention

Faraway stars
 and bygone blades of grass;
Soft lint
replaced the down
 of demolished feathers;
 a modicum
    resting

Beneath a mass of brazen toes
and prodigal feet

Panes of glass will do nothing
to hide the size of falling rain
 or catapulting stones,
against grand sheets
of impacted persona
and colloquial mutterings

The breath of freedom
is little more
than the rendering of moon heaven;
urbane inclination
 and provincial dates,
determining the course
of unnatural event
led before pre-empted disaster.

UNWRITTEN ARTICLE

¡The news today! made
            no exuberant headline-/
     (···despite
resonant howls of unrest-/

War torn
market rugs
and spilled mothers' milk
left stains
in upholstered crevices
and upheld noses

We were politically correct
in those mathematical
calculations
in which we tersely stated our
subliminal manipulation
of scientific theories
that had thrown out all fact
in favour of Intuitive sources
And adamant reckoning --]

the Cat
chased after the dog today,
instead of it being
the other way around
Now the dog
is a little confused

His power is seemingly
a trifle diminished,

and the kitten is meekly proud
of her newest achievement
So we scared the crowd again
Whilst they sat watching
the television—
(unconsciously) hampered
by waveless happenings /And
.........bland assessment.

THE LAST TOY SOLD

= =
sculptured wood = = =
= = =
Touch-ups
had us biting into grooves
   (and scrutinising price tags)

graft on™
  the prodigious trademark

Wait, while I ask my
financial advisor
if we're
spilling over the investment
rim;
Weightlifters
pounding kilograms
into pockets
*($*Costliness takes up
 the most time of fools)

Your stubbly needs
are creating sales tax,
burnished funds exposing
shiny merchandise
[on a wholesaler's whim]

scuffed faces;

their
intelligence is down-trodden
Upturned pride got
redistributed—and Santa's
sack is bursting,
He can't fit down the
chimney,
  so depressed from last years'
milk and cookie (→ with no one paying
frank service charge),
Wishing daddies would find
alternative aspiration
So that disconcerted children
are not left wanting glossy
hospitality, or new arrivals

Above the crib,
[they knew] the hideous dollar
was effecting Nick's lassitude.

CHINESE WHISPERS:
POEMS IN TRANSIT

MOVING STATUE

successful poetry
began
with the Star of David

his caricature stood
in the middle
of a fountainhead,
darting
between shadows
and flickers of saints,

stitching sinners
into dishonest possessions

Patches of light would
perambulate the fringes
of stealth and supposition

No one knows quite how many
bare-chested men
have been dismissed
in lieu
of pragmatic identification

They are there somewhere,
dancing among
short-term bravery,
casting

glances at sideways origin

mama wiped a clean gash
The faces
of her ghost-pale sons
idling between
bundles of frightened daughters

[snickering bookstore]

SCENARIOS

In a flimsy economy,
belt-tightening
makes perverse sense;

Before we turn over
ineptitude
to the stoic hands
of an authority,
we would do well
     to first retrieve
a tiny piece of the loot
as keepsake
of our sanity—

Polished mirrors
  (looking for pin-tuck)

We worked,
if only to fritter away;
We gave over bride,
   so as to recycle the system
through scant regeneration

(likely, she missed the point)
tykes knocking over
wooden building blocks
in the grand hope that
they will

stand up
by themselves

Easy click of the finger;
repatriation pushed to one side

send Father figure home—
tomato soup is steaming
with floating alphabet
and marital disharmony

Who's home from War?
Why didn't Peace wipe his feet
on the welcome mat?

JAMAICAN GENTLEMAN

Negro
transmuting from a

walnut shell—
show us
your ultra-violet tan

moored in the
harbour of white souls,
bleeding blue and
black;
flaxen animosity
permeates under hardy
skin
Still, he feels the
concealed breath
of apprehension

Who *are* you?
Defy me—
deny
that I wish no harm
I am only the colour of soil

your feet
step on me unwittingly
Then turn over
terrestrial compliment

and ruddy assent

fissures
splitting in rosy company,
[cleft] tilling the same Earth

like-minded gene pool
sell the farmer's wife
(It's hybrid auction day)
and she's flabbergasted
by the

illiteracy of mixed species.

JUNCTION

Shortly,
      we will administer
   in gradual
succession,

   a hygienic description
 of irremissible
causes, as to why our
shivering counterparts
are dying

our sun-tanned physician
has remedial intuition;
his gut feeling suggests
that perhaps our solar panels
are not receiving enough
good and wholesome sunshine

Brashly, we respond with
ragged indignation (···
his best oration will know
how to probe any weakness)

The children went to bed,
so we could get them up early
and shout in their ear—
they only have one drum

cry as we might,
 our tears aren't listening
Inexorably,
the condemned child
is extremely puzzled by the mirror
'I too, am immaculate', he thinks

But as yet, the social ecologist
has small voice
against devout psychotherapy
and strident ministers

please update the church file
(and briskly)
We are accelerating pedestrians.

AKASHA

in spite of fifteen rosaries,
go figure

why I lost my head
over emotional infidelity,
why the network of nicety
did not take out an insurance policy

I was not able
to rectify in time-space those
nihilistic tenets of mine;
 God's turf:
He made lawn bowls
of the ocean floor, exhuming
a plenitude of players

Such an obstinate game—
didn't they realise
that sand under their toes
was
scattering selfishly?
stingrays playing tennis
whipping tails to see who would win

Of course, nobody
would loiter around
sharks too long—too dangerous
to be enduring grey;

Nurses
peeped their heads in/
 /- now and then/
to check on terror
Mermaids blowing bubbles,
giving men the signal
to shoot them quietly in the back
with tacit speargun,

nought hits today—
inter-cultural misfires;
the recklessness
of effervescent youth
(token gamble)
Displayed massacre.

TREE-FELLER

Mother
you're the *nicest* bird
but the walls of your nest
are poised
too high to be
[unconditionally] touching

   :) measured age
is where
the ruler is in sight

Then they
edited the final jump—
inconsolable wings
hitting the pavement:
a sigh of relief, siblings clap
more worms
add to the food

sautéed twigs at play
The brunch has been
laid for zesty remonstration

white-collar doctor
skips away
from another confrontation
with missed breakfast,
suitably re-directing

next morning's schedule
away from factory floor
 (day-after is always a good sign)

working class prey:
he's worth a lot of money
Big Eagle is a hairless man
scraping the sky, mopping the labs
Not surprisingly,
the baby
is blushing

birdcalls survived another downpour
(a flux of mother's temperament

and cumulus mood)

SYMPATHY BOAT

garbage is the filth
of rejected emotion~~ ~~
~~ floating market,
Floated dollar
and odious by-product

we've made a [hypothermic] plea
to follow the guidelines
of our latest currency
& quintessential dress-styles,
Mortgages
tailored to threesomes

discreet submarine sank
too low in liaison
Vice-captain's view
is wide and farthest
(can't get out
of this space cab),
 although tank
 is
two-thirds airless,
oxygenated fuel should not
be seeping melancholia

trucker
has steering wheel stuck to
miniature hands

his discerning grip is slipping,
laundered fist trying
to pick-pocket
better affirmation;
≈ gossamer eyes open
velcro eyes closing,
decimal point registers
the variance [with a blink]
infra-red warnings—
underwater sprinters

Fluid circuit [pulverized ground]

EXCAVATION

[To Whom It May Concern:]

? ¿ who assigned licences
to those of feeble character

to be delegates of
rigid criticism?
[in effect, we reside in a
playhouse of hillbillies]:

the sensory arcade taps into
moral corridors,
where the wisecrack
stirs a voluble retort;

Second-class negligence
found its way
inside of titanic mansions;
Spiral staircase
got us lost again and again
on the climb back up
lighthouses into
godforsaken territory

trinkets sprawled over carpets,
covered in nostalgic dust
Came across an irate landlord
(where's his leading lady?)

What if ···every ship sank···?
An elusive submarine
had taskmaster envisaging
the depth of the breeze,
but its occupants would
no doubt elope too hastily

Skipper runs a mean fleet
army absconded
Not a moment too soon,
that granules
would disappear down plug-hole.

NEXUS

Religiously   (*p l e a s e*)

shall we donate our
overhanging escapades
to a more Practical cause?

those devotions
once flaunted, now
seem phlegmatic
to everyday speech
(agrees an antipathetic public)

currently,
my cut-out heart
is rasping
The Aztecs took over;
yet another civilisation
bites the dust;
 insatiable playwright sinking
his loveable teeth

 into vibrant commission

inertly, I thought of a freckle,
after that
the smallest billiard
And will you flex your pride?
(it's diminutive, as well)

bisected pen pals
find that autonomy is unbeatable

Deploy ⇨ a non-stop ⇨ conciliation
of brethren
in low profile neighbourhoods,
But steadfastly—the piping
is moving clumps of racial distaste
Further downtown.

GUSHING FOUNTAIN

Night owl)
  releases trepidation)
all at once)

his compelling messages
fiercely sting the eyes at
receiving end   *[: curse*
those dastardly bedwetters] :

She gathers the cow-parsley
at first crop,
unclothed and waterlogged,
espadrilles once-royal
needing urgent repair

Summers dry,
  (regarding dying roses)
though
bright thorns continuing
to thrive
at
glamour's insistence, having
mustered new alliances

put down the pleasing knife
Ouch, she's cutting
into woodpiles
with a ravenous axe;

check out the menagerie
of collectable zoo specimens
(with peculiar sideburns)

balsamic brain-waves,

Drawn from the faculty
of personal memoir,
insensitively
skewed—to the likes
of
ogling fishermen.

NUMBERLESS

a
disputable subset: *yes-equals-no*
(St Andrew's spider consents to
 playing noughts and crosses)

they will eliminate themselves
by default,

···being (foolishly)
attached to their enterprising

Switch-over
to politesse/

a
detestable signboard has the
sign-writer on tenterhooks,
 Stockists
featured in grouchy sequence

Castor and Pollux
are inseparable,
their circle of support
controlled by an industrial
backbone;
"Publish and Present"
The Ultimate Guide to
Consumption

[=for viewing through
perspex only=]
illuminated celebrants
directing their own movies
with blind videotapes,

dubbing offenders & litterbugs;
ejecting a
manifesto of baited speeches

TV programmes flattened
between pages
 of promotional offers
and benign hocus-pocus;
mottled faces, blotchy breakdown
   Elastic stance
witnessed (∞ swirling) infinity

Saving time—
is actually building up
longest journey.

SAGE

Found myself

one
lime pigeon in a
frugal spot of bother,
 employing
purgative wordplay
between a gasbag
and a brigand;

rushed letterboxes
remind me
that the mailman is
coming
(acrimony is flagged:)

What does the frontier
signify?
the haze lifted, so we're
reviewing the graffiti
at every stopover—
a fantasist on excursion

roaring cult
takes up lengthy strides;
seasoned improvements
on social home front,
radiant shop displays

include
premeditated affection
and ceremonial chitchat

Penman experimenting
with curiosity
recovers the fact
that nobody digs up
entire archaeology
and studies date-lines

Except perhaps
the kleptomaniac,
 dirt thief
finds all bones
and still-warm chatter

Tooth enamel is
cheaply traded
by head-hunters, [Erratic quota]

discarded fragrances
This company carries tag of
poisoned ethic.

MEMORABILIA

Let's rewind
to the absolute beginning:
we've got a
nauseating hunch
that
he's digging up the square
Sniffing out regal fragrance
 (where the sandpit
has been watered down)

mosey on over to
the Family Tree—
 he's mordantly pulling on the leash,
with the human off-spring
being admirably garnished

better that
a stranger does you
favour, than to be
constricted by the collar
of control
(---& didn't we all gnaw at
those acclaimed slippers---)

the difference between
sooner and later
is simply that the dead
are waiting longer

to creep out of ambiguity,
and share satirical smiles

Towering palms: the hand
is outstretched
to be bitten ↘
knuckles should be made
wary, since rage
is conducive to stagey
exploits,

Then they will
never decipher the whine.

SIENNA

global historians
wearing nothing but glasses,
   Thick as night,
impart foggy adaptations
tinted with reciprocal hues
   // Wish we could see
beyond those boroughs
of parochial encumbrance

diverging from zenith
and into
straightforward contrition
I'm thankful
that I brought along
my own scoop of sundries
(might I drag my sullen grave)

tonight will
bury my black heart
Diamonds, Clubs—
and the rest of
that bulky deck of cards
wrapped in velvet earnest

we put away dogma
(too early we think,
since it had not yet
finished barking)

relapses are common
We are folk too flippant
to recognise
the supreme length

of this intoxicating expedition;
  groundbreaking perspiration

[hyperbolic dogleg]

ssshhh···Catch up to fraying hem.

FATHER

Aquarian—seen conversing
with a lemon tree,
wherein he describes
the sour Passages of time   .. ..
----|-| --|
Glorified dead-ends:]
last jaunt
had the odometer truly fooled;

(traipsing around in circles)
Weren't you

lined up with worry
and creased into edges
Folds
and folds of crinkled moustaches

longing souls
and Heaven's stumpy legs
(the mirror hereby stabilising)
unprompted clouds
toil after whimpering puberty
Take note of arrogance, since
he is also the jockey of self-pity

grain-fed woman
is overjoyed—

countryman
put down his callous arms

Before her blood was milked.

GUARDIAN

The fanatics were right,
but with them all
screaming within earshot

I couldn't grasp
the edge
under those words

it looked like some sort
of innovative seafood,
mixed cocktail maybe
and madeira cake

What *was* that recipe?

why won't
they remember me,
now that they gave
such bombastic advice?

baroque qualities
bore an equal label:
the homemaker's lesson

Any refunds
On a ticking clock?
purchase receipts
must be made out

unequivocally to all consumers

A pearl-coloured prospectus
is required to share
in the anniversary of funds

quarterly statements
attracting
edacious annual penalty

hidey-hole of babes
rocked to Christmas tunes
(swell savings)

The Court pays all expenses.

IRON ORE

I've gathered raw deposits,
 child
with like mind

dug up a modest-sized
Angel,
covered in darkish flecks

and mouth full of grit;
It was succeeding to escape
 the absurdities of wealth,
Earth gone mad
over land-locked promise

Rubbing ice-cream
into
the palms of hands,
 As if cancers would dissolve
so easily···

they've unloaded scraps
with industrious aversion
The outpatient might perish
where nation's libido is leaning

radioactive plasma
dried organs
>> sending to South America

by snail mail

(safely,
spontaneously even)

warped transmitter
Remove, please—your hard hat
prior to entering worksite

excavations will continue,
until

they have blown up every mind.

NARCISSUS

Protect these fields
from intrusion
 into
thin-skinned territory,

Flowery symposium
nuzzled in ambrosial bushes
   /tenderly evading
the insidious click of a camera

hypersensitive eyesight
sees lens inflecting to
align with the Perfect Self

Right side feels
a touch prickled,
 although we handle the pipsqueak
with care—
Out-of-range scythe;
Rows and columns meet
tempestuously
in the centre (between
huddling exhibitionists)

a sentient
deposit box / shows altered records
the Foliage shovelling
whitish petals

in carnivalesque spite

watch now, while they're
dropping crimson dagger
The Seedling⋯

⋯she grew big and tallest
Dad so proud
of his spade; I apologise
if I am kindly protruding
(with lizard-like imposition)

naiads are lulled senseless
Tree sprites in
perched sentry.

EMPORIUM

masque of
accomplishment:]

We
don't *own*
this enclosure
(besides the merry-go-rounds)
a lone bus
stops out front of vortex,
vacuuming
large quantities of space
and gobsmacked brood

Dusty floorboards
lift up to reveal
mites (crawling
cobwebs)
and slow-learners

 ingenuous placement
 of junior love nest

I look better as
a star,
simple job
to shine without
adapter

-/anabolic faction-/-spending-
 slovenly cash

Emulsified journal
markings
···morgues
the milky grave of
plastic surgeons.

TRANSLUCENT PROMISE

press-box

will rebuke the matriarch
[upgrading the stakes
 of her Responsibility]

All the while her joy blooms gaily,
accompanied by the
majesty of wonder
and pagan adulation- - - - - - - - - - - -
Elevate.
Yet in the chamber of
Glory's heart
rests a murmuring dissension

Man is not woman,
though he glimpses her
(off the cuff)—*& in Still Life*

incandescent blessing
grants him pithy recompense
(a husky voice -- heard on doomsday)
pull-out shunned idols
from their weekly catalogues;
take respite in dubious drinking-songs
and blundered drum roll;

a reversed appraisal

talks of self-loathing,
but this IS my body;
 disquiet is hankering
to subside—

another bout of reaction,
 narcotic for closet tedium;
Sagged concerns
becoming less important

in these ageing times
  (resumed questions)—

Yes, I'm listening…

DOGFIGHT

Domestic combat has
wings tipped

in favour of the
dodo bird—who sits
indiscreetly watching the
shadows of his extinct judgement,
jeering at
dismantled affairs

ground support
is
trudging wearily
Flight operator's manual
remembered no sooner than
they'd woken up in brightest alarm

(don't worry,
you're neither dead yet, nor sleeping)

asinine buzzer
Trivial demand to call
another harebrained orderly
Appendix
has been shot in [which] side?

scruffy faces
grimacing in absentia

Put my coat on—
warm against the cheating wind
frantic slipper
and
a fuzzy newspaper

Grandparents lived long enough
⋯not to argue
about who would feed the babysitter.

HAIRPIN

laconic reasoning placed
 in
pocket-sized guestrooms;

actuality
   rests slender
against facial impressions,
whilst we are stripping conviction
And duping multiplicity

Geniality
is draped carefully
around bared shoulders
Tight waists
and loose belts

presumably, entertainment
doesn't come cheap these days
Or does it?
we should be duly advised···

   ···Of the folding of adulterated linen,
& of exotic love potions downed···   )

The melting of tongues
inside hors d'œuvres,
snaffled from an alternate platter
   and cut into

       self-sufficing quarters
    [enamelled seating:]
~/sited in the Ministry of Reputation/

Gently rouse the follicles of effrontery
Chestnut wig
does lightly tease the grey fool,
Woman, too—is rejuvenating adrenalin
of heartless lust.

CONVERGING TRIBES

take original content to
merge interactive lovers—
they will
kiss &
make up

(I'm recalling giddiness)

Volcanic basin
drops
crudely into the continental
shelf of smallgoods; cut-rate nosh
bought by
unconstrained diners

Through
and throughout: {open the lid at
an inviolable perimeter}
You are entering an impeccability zone···
But protective footwear
must regularly be worn;

those treading
nonsensical waters
make phony excuses
to build new islands
of fun-packed slumber
for their slapdash clients

(best that we avoid imbroglios)

hackneyed runners
distributing out of date news;
Overdevelopment
can't leave alone
the lava, bloody integers—

within epicentres of
reluctant change,
we tie up lackadaisical spirits

into panoplies
of scrabbling Regress;
lunacy
reproduced around happy
rims, terse
confirmation of travel
 estimated bookings
(in this wilderness of agents)

SLANT STRIDES

custodian

agreed
to pull weeds
with exceptional haste
The accidental
yank—of flower

[tortured deity]
Aphrodisiac is found
in the midst of unpacked occasions,
dispensing in tepid water

Sold dwelling: that delusory cave
had hefty rent,
after which a
time-machine plunked
 inscrutably in my way

[adverse
Fatigue]:
a
multitude of twenty-something men
try hard
to climb to the ledge
of middle age
(their upmost memory obscured in
history's carving)

teacher skipped class; a period
of ancient rest
Does wonders, doesn't it?

Abstinence of mind
can never be taught
and the indolent
Enjoy the squalor
of dappled introspection

while brave
suffer the crush [in cocoon of events]

HEXAGON

I'm a little confused
inside five walls—
this Pentagon of Contrition;
perhaps the appearance
of an extra face
may shed
another dimension of light

I demand an elongated border
with lengthened pinafores
and decadent
padding
around the knees, minus
a stitch or two

I can see anarchy fitting into
push-ups
and limbering bandits
whose cantankerous muscles
& unmitigated corruption
retain infamous supplements

Lilac shrub:
the lavender is pensive
.. .. (.. .. *think I can* minutely pick up
the radar of another insect.. .. ..)

three plus one railwaymen

discerned the faintest
hint
of a building—
lightweight barracks
hitting them square in the belly

Valley of livestock;
a presumptuous sundae

I scream
to Assume

meltdown.

OWNERS OF PROCESS

Contrive a Kitchen Tea
 [a mock-up version]:

reputable trends deleted
and brand managers
in crosstalk: say hello to
the greedy middleman
(and his best men)
skinflint
father, Son, and
Holy team;
predecessors made
an abominable valuation;

Economy class
sent off its representatives
Bon Voyage
and all that:
come back in light years
(when you're simon-pure)

an inoperative schedule (%)
He as the proverbial dreamboat
and She in a swaggering nightdress,
 departing on
a ship of sailed tendency
and cruising overdraft

(Hire the disabled loan shark
with a pacified business plan)

bedraggled flag was put
in wrong location
common-sense chose
another way around;
deviations
quite clever (in knowing
what we don't)

amateurish problems—on a
serving dish
and dad takes it all home to his
gentle reclining chair,
his doting children (and
wife's chest, mimicking breast)
Silicon repairs
can wait 'til weekend.

RELAPSES

astringent judges
      leeching away the
restlessness
  of Wind···

[hush]··· a sharpened vibration
carries further··· ···

hand-picked sunflowers
are incriminated, Insofar as we
play against the comportment
of blustery accusation
and
distorted input

the reddest heart displays
a black centre, even as
they are auditing rainstorms

leaves emblazoned
with russet austerity, enrobed
 in
crumbling biodiversity

tuneless wind-chimes
are dispersing the
breathless mercy of mania—
heightened by

the levity of Happiness;

···Can't concentrate so well
around inbred conclusions

we didn't like all those staid men
togged up in
inhospitable overcoats; [blip]
Scatty discourse
Of shepherds who'd lost composure
where they'd borrowed a good time

Influential intruders
  keep ambience tame, yet
somehow wicked

ebullient Solitude,
the Elixir of egalitarians.

KHAKI

Those who had nothing better
 to do,
bought plastic—

production runs
boxed in willful individuals,
pen worship
 pencil shavings
Connoisseurs
enwrapping potential
from cellophane substitutes

Hard-wearing—is
   as easily breakable
      ((⋯and so we replace
the teething-ring)

churlish sum
versus noble reward

pseudo display
coming down with oozing symptoms,
 ( ) Recruited
pistol shoots at feisty mosquitoes
in bush territory; docudrama
shows meek depictions
of a mollycoddled landscape /≈/
townsfolk blissfully empowered to

search in the region of circulating
 (albeit artless) temptation
-- (: --

untitled scent
of an unnamed candle
Will I make a prayer?
Or blow out another grief-stricken wish?

tribute starts over;
the bleary soft-soaper shall
make amends—
restore her bubbling excitation
Keeping bête noire in sedate concealment.

BLACKOUT

Seer signed an affidavit,
being quickest to
elucidate the main point

Blame
the roasting scapegoat
for demon catholics

 and spitting embers

expiating columnist; he's
protesting about
the reign of
Diabolical intersections

[Spinifex—
still competing
with the gaiety of sand;

overblown suspicions
would attack the Investigator's plan]

plausible beginnings:
familiarise yourself with
interior lodgings, cutest maisonettes
and an all-embracing carapace

mental illness

is swaying like candlewicks;
we fix depression with new addiction
Then percussion starts again

ethnocentric clouds of combustible
dust
flammable dreamers; ad lib
explosion of suspended particles,
mutated
shapes of European clay
surmounted denial—& acerbic allegation
(we are committed to the brim)
september blacklist
Mystical repetition of the sixteenth century

time the wind

MY CONDOLENCES

I'm sneezing burdens
    onto
        the weathervane,
And they're expelling in
four awkward directions;

Thereafter the blood
of coagulated humanity
reads a quotation chosen
from the harried array
of dramatists, amassed
with
death-defying agility,

with the lexis expected
to take hoarse effect—/

Pay attention!
It refers to:
The pharmacy of fugitives
choked by the emphasis
of scientism attempting
to
prescribe a different route
to that which nature
so divinely intended

[-as denoted by

the memos of
travail and travesty-]

presenting then in contrast-
an infiltration of escapees
and pilfering outlaws,
grading high-voltage results
from brainpower and vitriol

But the thunderstorm is drowsy,
It doesn't score so highly anymore
nightfall
has made them numb
with so many purblind resolutions

I've not time
for new phenomenon
I've not time to even
the score,
nor wipe the sheen from
my unrecognised brow

So Goodbye to you too.

MANDALA

Caught the tailwind of
       black-and-white fairy tales,

  and crossed the threshold
into an impassive habitat;

we can undeniably
choose—Beggardom,
or the steady chain-gang- - - -

aspirants wholly besotted
with preparations
(for passing) into tertiary awareness
demand the whereabouts of paranoia

alumni of soul-searchers
dangles from the ceilings;
litigation is rising,
but conventional law
is out-of-javelin-bounds

transcend the nominal hype:
 dynasties
built upon trampled sandcastles
and roly-poly persons

Dumped trucks; walking tracks
have already been mined

for alluvial potential-/

Rich tip to the
loyal waiter—
he earned his yard glass

The eleventh commandment
reads blank;
make it up as you go
Your head will count
a Thousand

more reasons to impress

blasted cannons;
jade buddha sits upon china wall
burgundy icon
[no infringement here]
cemented culture is deaf.

LEATHER FORMATIONS

I am clay soldier
Wet blanket

mummy undressed me—

I was boasting to say yes,
or they would have
eaten
me anyway

With a tinge of
tossed salad
and a twinge of winged guilt,
I'm now a morsel
worth every cent of society

What simulated nonsense!
you smile upon my naïve self
as the juice drips from
your
liquefied fingers

...itty bitty people can't
think of better words...

scruples withered,
Damn the pitch
of uprising fathers—

God will only bring them
down again

where mother can Coo
and sibling can squeal

Stop! knife and fork
is also foot in mouth
Banquet is first-class vocabulary
for a jewfish

Who else, is so clueless?

HOVERING PANIC

Their vulgar impulses
won't properly disband:

we are dream-weaving
 in
a time-share tenement,
surrounded by
frivolous candles
and
blurry-eyed expenditure;

Sampled fabrics
   bartered bliss
God designed the lamb
to wear whitest

[rustic tone]
panache blade; flamboyant

slivers of a cut-throat world;
Sincerest eyes take
vulnerable note of what
is to come, (but Pandemonium
wears her own warning)
green apples dropping
indiscriminately in the box

we will make-do:)

choosing
not how to fall
but When to land…

The flight path has
served up new meaning;
where hands fumbled,
rigor mortis adopted control
A stiffened attendant
looks behind her shoulder
as the curves of her cheeks
become remunerated
Liquor cabinet
is a drowning mess; coffee beans
hiding in distilled waters
portholes to aqueous fantasy.

ORANGE EXPLOSIVES

here's a
  bevy
      of
          shattered bones,

indigestible concoction
 of
cloying youth
  [from our gloating school days]
Smorgasbord smiles
favourably on the widest menu;
scan the al fresco selection

syrupy grinners
drool at the prize-draw
Another schmuck
can taste unsweetened victory;
sugar-baby
  is the toughest, grain
to blame
the meat;
salt adds to the paste, or just to
blot out wasted memory
(can I have your remains?)

trampling vertebrates &
stampeding lolly-goers

------| Eye the kamikaze display
of gambolling confectionery |--------

curdled taste-buds
Love the
yoghurt flavours—party on
candied deck

In swarm the birthday clowns,
though Dad's gambled half
the entry price
Blocked doorways
stuck on partial smiles

Mustered joy,
and chronic tummies.

FOUNTAIN PEN

Word list
took too long
to reach the recipient

e-mail
 branded him dryly
with wry ink

dried up relation;
 comparing notes by scrimpy
font

dehydrated feather
carries messages
Like a pigeon—
homing;
homily
Or honed instinct

Birdcages corresponding to
gruesome humour
(and they're all tittering)

unscrambled eggs minus
cold toast and burnt coffee,
caffeine rushing out the door
to circumvent valuable losses

Of time; Interlocutors
with hourglass figures
[- all-of-whom -] look alike
by my squarish bankbook;
Glossaries
conjuring a dual definition

[balding] gratitude
sends two ways.

EXTRACTION

fortified tuition & training
 (and a
manual crassly supplied)

Zip files
to aid
the lumbering assets
of Computer—& sociable fitness

novice carefully abides by
the manufacturer's warning:
High intensity label
and paginated stickers

 : just out of stock :

Because we lived
underground,
it was hard not to
trip up on ferocious cables,
whilst they skied
overhead,
bored with their
parallel universe

Disheartened,
we couldn't drag conduct
to higher ground

with gunfire paid to ricochet

(urban) cliff dweller
is safeguarding the municipal shrine;
we celebrate gregarious insights
when the peaks hit
bottommost:
 sorest eyelids
 & towering lashes

Concrete statuettes
are looming in ugly shadows
Artistic glasshouse,
dig up the surface
to locate taurine gem.

UNSOLICITED

The repressed are dying
to express
a provident wish—

Mystery redeemed
in the clutches
of mawkish amateurs:
Seek out professional help
The controversialist
searching
for a bilingual place,
though none ever
mentioned in the want ads

A troupe of newscasters
carries the torch of
scathing recognition and
socio-economic discharge
Vapid scriptwriters
trafficking pages
of nationwide resources
in conjunction with
caustic layers of netiquette

we commune
with vagrant commercial
 [the simpleton never goes astray]
 And Asia is ever

the composite of Eastern soliloquy:)
westernised glove puppet
acting before throngs of cameramen;
I beckon
that the compass falls my way
Show a fading star that her
abstract variations still solicit appeal,

Or at least, the sophistication
of superimposed motif
[Slender frown]
pilgrims descend As we enter new territory.

RED AND PINK SONGBOOKS:
WASHED POETICS

THE SEA IS FOR SALE

We've sunk into
a beautiful kind
of depression,

[leaking mermaids]
She's cried
the whole ocean
dry eyelashes are linking
taut, snapping
under pressure
They will shudder in her
voluptuous embrace

Stepping stones to an abyss;
crustaceans
duplicating
  (these feedlots are ludicrously
overcrowded)

I'll have a
coffee on the rocks
and a dash of
undying civility;
Savvy celebrations:
who pulled down
the balloon?
[helium is waving]

chuckling sailors / frisking with
squatting girls in heavy black
T-shirts,
men with mnemonic fixations
skulking in the darkness
 tails slapping, and
naked eyes watching⋯
 Undulating misfits
bobbing in shallows   [betwixt
   evaporating leisure]

The complacent shoreline
has begun to
mutilate prospect.

FUTILE SCISSORS

Divide
aptitude, but not carelessly

Eavesdropping
is not uncommon
within enchanted forests

fables
so real, gone past effeminate turn-off
Beckoning trespassers
to alight carriers
frequenting the Silk Road

caterpillars pacing themselves
to don loveliest costumes
Balloons jiggling
for the delighted onlooker

a dissipated transfer:
take the ferry across
grubby water; a
muddy tributary misleads to delta
[one part wet : two parts dry]

Waxing of the moon
subsides,
light is waning—and
daydreams are eloping

The enveloping twilight
scares all but one sedate follower
 Tiptoes
of a puppeteer

[excited warble]
snowflake—
lands upon the back of a bleating goat

IVORY BURROW

'I don't do anything
else except cry,'
said the little girl

my sweltering
blossoms
were forced to seize the trellis
under false agreement
'I'm only tiny,' she
daintily sighed,
vines wrapped tightly 'round wrists

tripping ankles:
mad men
sauntered past outlandish hordes

In a barrage
of lost question,
the ultimate answer can't even
remember
  [ask pugnacious husbands]

inoperative
ensemble—enacting
detached moods
for latecomers

ample room

in this all-purpose space
[between the pillars of fortified asylum]

Timed chronicles,
daisy speaks in timid voice
Alliteration
is simplest speech
Easy to repeat (where one knows
to comprehend the inner language)

christmas bells;
we need manager to coach sound.

DAYLIGHT

Hippie drunk too much
wine, danced
around too many
flickering candles

Drank
and masqueraded
with the most fictitious
characters
An acidic brush with death

droning catchcry
of a transformed wasp:
listen out for
short-lived sensation   ))···
(vicarious settlers)
who was it that said so?

He thinks she's a butterfly—
She knows there's a fly
in the butter

[odds-on] groped torsos,
another dissected abdomen
Unglamorous leaf—
but it's their only home;
double-breasted carport,
with plenty of room

to sleep
 (I mean, sweep)
between sleeping bags

lapel is ripped
import
Overseas box; Fragile crate
with a platter of quaking content
pick
and choose—
limitless choice is suited
to guests lolling
with champagne; flute glass
is best instrument I can play

(forgive me;
I'm just green frog
with croaking throat)

AMPERSAND

Angelfish
And
(an angel & fish)

Swimming
between the seas
of twelve startled apostles;

  On the fourteenth rock
    we sit,
nursing dire templates
  and ill-disposed tempos,
It's nobody's melodrama

  [look at]: benign grains
  of coarsely sifted sand

blow-dried murals revere
an eye-catching cremation
  Gorgeous roads hugging
picture-perfect rock-faces

but the sand dunes, Hitherto
wish to stretch out for
another millennium,)reaching to
millions of starving sun-lovers   )

  subterfuge of grasses; pleated towels

and clothing draped lazily,
while we wade
through the tangle of
contemporary credibility towards
 a statement of
burnt belief; Creed is reeled back.

SOFTENED SKETCH

Scenes in the darkened
foreground, like so:

Sooty visitors leaning over
the lovers' Balcony,
contesting an extraordinary deck
that extends for miles
   and miles, reducing to
kilometric centimetres
Am I confusing your function?

raise the quotient
to superscript,
I'm the power of four—
even with one crucial component
missing
 clip-on thumb [flanking]
broken index finger,
subtract the common-jointed wrist

Obligations find my skinny pencil
immortalised in
gargantuan manifestations,
stocked up on luxurious carat

They won't find me
canvassing for
the insoluble mathematician,

I've finished the pictures in
my three-tiered application

Call now the gofer—get him to
wrangle more staples
from the centrefold

Bona fide furnishings stand out,
because they sat me behind barbed-wire
until I could articulate
proper drawing;

[no fixtures]
no pastel
Just bold exploits.

ALTRUISTIC CROISSANT

(((((spiritualism
mixed in with strawberry jam)
soggy sandwiches
are best
if
kept away from
hungry diggers, prowling
for milk-cartons & free topping)-

A cookie is all I need
to revive
the apricot chicken

Tuscany-inspired
crater ash,
adobe brick
& melted pavers from
the cobbler's roiling endeavours

Affections bought and sold
Servility mildly exchanging hands
(it all tastes good to the chilli pepper)

yes, we'll come back later
we promise,
[before the Toast gets cold]
capitalised
the first letter

(so you'll believe us)
Dear sucker,
Religion is deluding you

Prick that diabetic finger
to drain excess blood-sugar

cursory illness

The memory game.

PATRIOT LOVER

That night
I came and pulled you
out of the sea;
The moon rang twice,
 dusk turned over an early sunset

loquacious seclusion
Still thoughts,
dredged from a thinking past
(naïvely lost in sullen traffic)

Naturalism
was a state of mind,
Hurricane heaven
Torpid bliss—accommodating
pellets of hard rain

My transcribed rites of passage
and the gap that made
      befitting segments
in your unruly heart

An outline
a general plan;
The risk of never
The thrill of ever again

Happy returns

heady memories
Chilling prophetess was my
inspiring teacher

Did we call each other?
Or did the game perhaps
begin
to scratch new numbers
inside a chalky constellation?

GEOMETRY

[-
-inaugural-] square dance:

Seasons introduced
by
the cycles of sympathy
Saturation of arid skins
incurs a languid sarcasm,

with gullible circles most
susceptible to
splotches of sunspot—even
cloudless brilliance
shelters his depression
under bluest hue,
averting to
ambiguous wastelands

Testing the sun once more
for approximate contrasts
 and redolent mannerism;
Life-force seeps out from
every courtyard, along with
the heady odours of
staff unloading cargo
by the guesstimated hour

we triangles

are turning dizzy,
with summer in revolt
and autumn already
despising⋯
(Rise to life-size animations
or else, a heckling suitcase)

Aromas
of miscellaneous regret:
Early tragedies now the rule
for measuring discoloured
dialect
A week-long vacation
made weaker, more tired
We sit amidst the mined gold—
resembling dust
  and opals who never
eventuated
to be defined as necklace.

HAIKU

The rules were sharply ignored
when
seventeen syllables

populated
to fit beyond a page,
Yet the fibres of expression
stayed firmly
entrenched,
For the air of mind
had no place to compress
except onto infinite sheets

of crisply embroidered
rice paper

unconfirmed cherry blossoms
were moored
next to origami boats,
Their contours inscribed
with talcum-white modesty,
Emerging
to produce a myriad
 of élite interpretations
amongst literati and stage crew

The stems of vowel-sound
are pre-booked

by every written innuendo
Vital statistics accentuated
 and shrouded
by winter's tincture

Infected leaves
 smile nevertheless, while devices
insert captured attention.

HITCHHIKER

Will you
please get me to paradise?

Tow truck broke down,
bicycle sports a flat tyre
and the back of the utility
has been taken up
entirely by the pooch
      (faithful as she is)

get out of my way
Get me high
got myself uplifted
by a kind
policeman—
mighty, with dashing grace
Off duty
but congenial nonetheless;
he says that these new roads
are boasting scenarios
      and mongrel scenes

Death traps the plaintiff:
in this
planetarium of flesh, we are
staring at chunky pieces
 of razzle-dazzle and ratings,
petitioning payment

for no-frills anatomy XX
[Independently, we admit that the
TV reports better with spectacles]

so now we can poke, prod
—and pamper
the rascal pimp tonight
We think it's his turn
to be the butt of shame,

This way
young girl stands a small chance.

ISTHMUS

like the South-West wind,
Off-shore poet
senses when the crone is swelling

hasty crossings delayed
and retracted;

(along the) horizontal island:
I can
just touch
the narrowest strip
of land,
which
my leaning likelihood
has never before seen—
Overseers of settlement
took over the removal
of kindred supporters
(we are paupers in hiding)

Stop
wringing my neck

...without drippiest publicity,
conservatism sticks to
handrails—
snail
 stuck to a glass-bottom vessel

barefoot surfer
hit the sand with his nose, whence he
smelled foreshore roses
together with the stench of rotting kelp;
 Insubstantial mist,
marshes in lieu of an ocean—
please use a rubber glove
Have you ever breathed a word?? yes, *Reality*
 (that word
wrongly bestowed on the weary)

They all commanded guttural excuses,
 grassroots of hustled impulse
Appeasements···[part of the tidal ritual]

SALT CRYSTALS

Sweet attention
mixed
Haphazardly
with lumps of superfine minerals
and
colorific residues ¬

SCaffoLD
and reinforcements
afford standing room
for the womaniser
!Ahem! [But for the ladies]
Sweat shops are likened to
Internal chambers
of peremptory brain space
and stanch cavity;
unyielding rays
of laid flame, and laden spark

Rose water
Glistens upon airborne petals,
 A shrine of garden lilies
streaked
with the dimness of
Evening lanterns,

loopholes
and crossed wires

sea swept couples—licking dew
from briny lashes
Herbs and crushed peppercorns,
Feigning taste
for the sake of a vow,

mussed up shards
are fusing...

accosted flakes
detained on rash approach
 (tip out the tourist's knapsack)
The wind lifts a palm frond,
like a lost hand

My constant brow
of frowning width
is just out of thrilling reach.

RED SKIES

hack:) foreign hunter
sinking his teeth
into soiled words

eggs got side-tracked
(we don't kindly say so)
Capricorn stays
in the
noiseless background;
The enlightened poet

is spry companion,
Discretion is his friend
he turns
her inclining head

...so they are joined
at the buttock

she wishes / he grants
 she declines,
for need of
more fortunate circumstance

(I'll do my Way
by the morrow)
I am life, she says, not object
tea leaves sipped

from the baby's teacup

Chamomile forest
and ginseng root

water is energy, Tao
 [only so much muck
he
can swallow]
subsisting on paraphrases,
(her actions spilling hot oil)
That no light bulb could early detect.

SITAR

Pardon our faith; it missed
a beat—
    We momentarily
ran the ground line
to the wrong earth,
        preoccupied
--- - -
    --- --- ---
  with despotic soundtrack,
fixated on spasmodic alphabet

Then an auditory masterwork
ascends for the audience
and...
Ever After
configures a peaceable rhythm,
Remissive lines
 and buffed ambiance···
[recounting] sculpted music,

 whose soft deliberation
raises genteel notion,

sensitive yearnings
and decorous perception;

Nautical movements
in a

crusade of rollicking numerals
 : [The itinerant empire :]
Indian ocean
wrapped in Atlantic basin
alpha waves affording coverage,

 'til we find the crossroads
of bordering flat seas

and transverse winds
Shapeless plains
breeding an uncertain pilot.

PSYCHIC TRILOGY

Showcasing the linguist:
most talented writer
of a precarious essay /

lofty works had every
buoyant testimony
omitting yet another
clause; one more
poignant episode
in this vexing chapter;
shall we be
outwitted again?

foundations stripped by
an experimental prose-|

The tools we used were just
highlights of visual story,
diffusing in our dream-time;

We are each diminished
by beefy competitors
Gluttons undercover
of calorific crimes—
best that eyes can see

Emperors, demoted demons
  (and) immodest thrillers—

maintain lively demonstrations

Through poor wages,
cultural diversity is downgraded;
they refused my subsequent
anthology: only one winner
per entrée (dessert
pays an additional spoon)

lacklustre horizons
won't capture their rock-solid distraction
Immigrants (seen trekking
on establishments)

DEPARTING

This moment
lends me a dime, but since
I'm not an American,
   ten cents
only creates the
probability of an Opportunity

Sabbath-tooth tiger awards
inexpensive fossil fuel on Sundays
   (or on any good-day)
With environmental jaws
advocating vocal warfare,
tenure picks another contender—
But we've only enough sunbeams
for two people,
[and Noah's boat is sinking]

morose deportment:
  Jupiter's moons span a glum
circumference- - - -

Next description shows: personas
following intrinsic streets—& then into
 a blocked subway,
The organs of donors
running out to book flights
  to sacrosanct destinations

That doorway has a fork;
Its fold-out frame has
been retouched;
 Just as well, because lately
there sees a
great urge to split assurance

(élan and flair)
⠀⠀⠀⠀slinking through⋯
Saturn's rings having lavishly
expanded waistlines

⋯*If only*⋯the fast-talking assailant
could plug up the gushing hole
of embarrassment of those
hoarsely belittled by loudspeaker,
Give the slacker honourable mention
for his long service
 [and relapsed job description]

We were doing well
by candlelight, the -[nocturnal desecration]

PRAISE

surface
sunk

forget-me-not
[magenta moonrise
on this
Omen
of mornings]

A submissive biography:
Innate stature
has yet to unfold

freefalling assumption
to crash into
parasailing remark;
print
on daily demand

bin of neglected virtue
is overflowing
with vices, and vicious heroines
Sagas—
are long-gone; phallic flowers
wilting from jilted hymns

Era
of cloud-castles

and padded snowmen,
Each with fat scarf, brown-nosing
on a summer's day

bless my hardworking bible, and
[Take care] the harangued priest;
Shaman standing down ···*just as*···
incurable mother takes another steaming puff
of herbal solution

Alpine outskirts;
this icepack··· is cracking.

THE BLUE ROOM

swapping colours //

Navy entices a
      keen opponent,
   (and not a pang
    of infidelity)
aquatic drops
spotting the walls

Art of garbage: We are
  processing feeling

sixteen saints
with suspicious hats
 seen
decorating the crowd
   [patrolling hysterics]
Sterile nuns venture
to penetrate the social fumes

Disciplined symptoms—
they want to bottle them
as curatives ⇨(see advert placed
on mendacious notice-boards)
The filaments are threaded
in vain
sagging pigments; and dogged
persistence leading to

premature estrangement

a verifying presence: Be aware!
Of the perishable choir of poets,
chic infatuations
 [an illustrated following did
censor by acute requirements]

abject couples in drab décor;
That's how a beast is—
black and white vision
(with a platonic mailing address)
unstipulated family
 of induced familiarity,
nice portraits getting drenched,

 and matted.

O-ZONE

[sea-haze]:   Epoch of
the
fifty-plus screensaver

we should be
 [priggishly]
Culling those companies
of malodorous intention

and mind that
you switch off hot water—

Please don't
rub too many rosebuds
 Petals fall out
easily (you didn't think)

crazed
Sun
He doesn't
see the plight
of topography burned in his way;
ambient man
shooting big stars
into a blackened sky

science of the
red dwarf: he enrolled in a school

for scampering asteroids

[laugh, my chlorinated child
God is chiding you]

speckles of
galactic dust:
globetrotters stepping onto the
biggest atlas with their
 consumable existence;
what a silly cluster of minds

squinting at sand granules
Analysing with magnified
knowingness,
globules of nothing—
pockmarks of man's bull's-eye.

SYLLABUS

we linger in public limelight,
 but as yet
no superb sightings of aliens

(Evidently, it hasn't rained—
and so the lads
kept on playing golf⋯)

The core of community
is half-hoping
 ecology has climaxed,
So that it might abandon
the planet in pursuit
of digital entertainment

Annoyed by reception
we couldn't receive,
our static hands were closed

pensions denied
Euthanasia pursued
 and erroneously branded
as evil choice
[prolong the ignorance,
                    what for⋯?]

the writer does not die,

≑ nor a painter lack reason
to live

thus one's hobby makes for a
perpetual outlay;
　Homemade feedback
infers a good enough
response, when lightly wrapped

deluxe candidates
 and an empty doctor's surgery

we Love the portable continent.

ALCHEMIST

A louvred ego

Air,
combining with drizzle and
smokers—

herbaceous cigars
compressed
into
vertical lines of
thoughtlessness, wafting smoke rings
and dirty napkin,
mop up the atmospheric runoff

Lordship has hidden
butts; rivets in the lounges
of the guests' accommodation
 (take for granted, that you
were not a permanent resident)

burned holes with
your resentment, didn't you?
The facts are··· [face-to-face]

we don't like you gibbering
over weird potions,
Doctor of Energy
count to ten—and over again

save some unconscious lives,
greasy facilitator (quoting
requisites of salutary massage)
What kind of mentor
is sailing
along the rubble of sea-waves?
(stop imitating my pioneering pride)
 piqued faculties; Motley explorers

The man who measured liquid,
His boat sank before mine; I was placidly
beside myself, rocking
on a placebo of swell-current
Deepest leagues, a shaky place for divers.

SNOWMAKER

He's trying
to break through his
own skin, feet first
[and sober]
she's blending the cocktail,
Icicles dripping

They're both
racing each other to the ocean

he's following the blueprint
for evolution (it's scrawled
under the soles
   of historiated footsteps)
while she learns to recycle
the improvidence of fairy tales

magic has taught him
not to force change, that seeds
will be propagated by
equanimous embraces

he is the mind of criterion
she is the Spirit coming
to rule over that mind;
he is the body of dexterity
she is the Spirit engulfing
nimble portion of that body

    and so they are balancing caution

She is the vision,
    planted by natural intention
He is the setback,
looming in the skirts of her resistance
(doleful control
is bustling to mature: rickety inclines

Mechanical ecology)

AMPHIBIANS

At the lake's edge
is a liquid
corner,

meshing
with surrounding
boundaries by permission
of tangents,   and cosmic sphere

lines caressing
angles criss-crossing
(Folds permitting)

···and remember··· the weatherman
is not always right—
So correct the rainmaker
who appears too graphically certain

pluvial complacency; oh, how
you make us cleave to a sodden brow

Storms of Ideology
pierce through the choral tranquillity;
pick off the tentacles
of squirming frenzy, [bolting terrain]

Relegate the means of escape,
  /lightning strike bids lowest position/

Wooden pacifist
damned conceit; Dropped

melamine utensils by mistake; although they
were only Interim belongings, where
we'd trod on the foibles of granted affluence

festivities—
 the drawbridge for
modern billboards.

PARANORMAL

~~[~~ dissing him so easily
was a gambling mistake]

As legend
    ventured off-season,
time-distant intruders
reclaimed the attributes of
Self;

He stepped through the
looking-glass
 in mid-afternoon
It's quieter then—
most of the others are tied up
in conclusion
(my name not given mention)

I've envisaged
a new topic: To promote
tongue-twisted discussion
about a probable myth
couched in blasé appointment
and stony altercation
(Now you can have a flutter):

Those tactile chandeliers
and the remnants
you left of morning

are waiting by my afternoon side,
my beloved musketeer
referring passion and assembling peril
(Are you still larger-than-life?)

when work merged
through architectural rockface,
I was standing there
Whole
hole
purring…

like a chassis without driver

Skeletons on the highway
Big graveyard Number 1
half-hourly, I look at the clock—
hoping minutes
will soon be meeting limousine.

CINNAMON EYES

Bastard child
 and
a woven loom on attic door

Carnal vigour: monogamy
wears on the outside of
loose zippers,
 corks that popped too early
(cranky mother
having had no chance to cry);

the
map
is fogbound, though
Foreseeable in the short-term

   ···where correlations
are stacked ahead,

[crab apples] hand over
a formidable explication;

Essence
is scratched, and on the key
is the Engraver's signature;

kinetic soul
motions roughly

to the card players below;

Kismet
(destiny, she resuscitates me)
a juvenile awakening
hair is knotty
Pull over—the
car seat sweats beneath
clammy thighs and halted joyride

We declare that the holiday of youth
was but a pulped dream
Romantic scrolls [thus re-inserted]

OVA

[Commercial playback:]
another cocktail
of solvents; we're glad
for turnovers of
manufactured beauty
and selected ostracism

long legs—
Fetch always
a good price
in the gene pool

body engines
running
in hydrogenated overdrive

a corpulent fuel pump
bamboozled
the station attendant
[Gasoline
had guzzled more kilometres]

logbook
mixed up the columns
 [and the racing rats finished last]

so we did a
sperm test: he would gladly

exchange his
shotgun for a crash helmet,
would it genuinely hurt less

Recite your alphabet
and stamp
the letters with somebody else's
good-natured approval
(since rating vanity
is always in style)
I'm far behind in locomotion, still searching
the world for beauty's secret

…that I know is found somewhere in
The oval universe.

AMETHYST

Formalities had us imprisoned
  by
the ring of engagement
  : (an inverted paradox)

These burly hesitations
keep obscuring the light

lucky rabbit's foot,
Pigskins—and
their sheepish childhood
met with Alice, who lost
her way in Wonderland,
 age-old countrysides
lounging in rightful repose;
   An espied jewel
submits a novel constituent!

Purgative black spot, solid
cuts heavy into sediment;
Under skylights, gleaming physiques
 are at once
unobtrusive and intentional

winter's dawn
is descending > yet
 how do we
tell Time

when to disembark?
　⋯ Distance is retreating
[and the spectrum is jubilant]
Condensation is prolonged, if
only for the viewer's pleasure

To the east rises the aftermath of West,
Avalon can be dimly
glimpsed
by a glinting autumn
　(ravens secreted in shadowy moors)
water dragons skitter across
vindictive rocks ^
　beyond further plateau, sits quiet estuary
　　　[low-key crocodile likes his chalet]
a personal invitation to
Vanquish—
the impersonal guest.

THE CHRISTENING

Hydrated mask:)

we were talking too proudly
and godchild
dropped a fountain pen
on the bedding
(couldn't see the lucid ripples)

Original
White space ~

blest hairlines: please, Father
stop
rinsing out
your paintbrush,

sullied bristles
make the holy water dirty

Horse's hair
is textured with mother's floral
reminiscence: femme fatales
 (all starring in death's row)

We dotted another
picture
at school today;
no, I'm not colour blind

I'll take off my glasses, not my clothes

exclusive white socks
 knitted cap,
fitted firmly upon
the crown of a credulous child

Teach us to be innocent—
my pastor's wrist is too tight
and Church's crucifix is bent,
he can't see through sliding doors

pouring out my heart
is hard work with broken veins.

RETROGRADE

the Four-legged performer
croons only in the plural—
  it's Dante's singing circus

ugliness won't weep
because
inside the blackbird
is a mangled heart
 Ego releases e
the gross challenges of
death
(united foreboding):
Steal into
those images of splendour

Visual Pacifist watches
in starkest observation—
his gun points at eye level,
Brows lowered, motionless,
 instilling
laudable commiserations

a
garden of ladybugs
guards my
academic centre,
constructing the neatest shield
that they can

galvanised casing:
Core values lost evermore to
   conspicuous canons;
Weasel advances
with brassy salute onto
the footbridge; Clear away the
suburban culprit
who communicates
false pleasantries like a
marionette   [in order]

To Redeem
the skills of original puppet.

AUBERGINE MOON

Impromptu eyes] conceive
of an irrational reflection—
gigantic musings
    consternating on
arterial diameter,
ruminating giant symptoms

Revelation breaks out with
stupendous pick-up lines;
Origin is obscured,
but smooth out
those frightened yearnings
in any case (: wailing dehydration)

Death is grazing
Sleepily
over bottomless tableland,
with her newest babe-in-arms

a vast rush
 of misgiving—is giving way
to landless conjecture,

birds illegally parked
under stars, like ghosts
smartly wandering,
Fleeting

associations
(and far-fetched glimpses)

The eternal sermon:)

Involuntary music:
wacky enigma
and bizarre portrayal;
 night-time
catches an easy light < >
         ··· *(&) If-One-Is-Knowing-*
Where-To-Look,
precise locations are adorned
with inane displacements

day by day vocations (peaking
at dusk)
beneath a miraculous rock.

SABBATICAL QUEEN

Call on Miss Impossibility,
   if your word length be
curtailed,
        or—truncated;

Impoverished allegiance
put self-Esteem in decline;
disentangled weeds,
   Sea plants thriving in the
outer reaches of ocean floor ∬-∬

Pluto takes a hiding—'cause
that's just the way
he likes his smacked leather
Whip
those bone-dry mortals
into doggoned obedience

The waterless planet
has nominated moonbeam:
See webpage for
genocidal tendencies and persons
to bathe away
the stellar townscape

Hey, what if I say 'I do',
and a terrifying sneeze
ensues?

will they dish out ruby-red
medicine, mercury & silver,
or some anaesthetised hostility?-?-?

Bundle spoon
into the mouth
Take child's astrological
reading—the
meter of temperament
and respectable compulsion;
replenish the board room
with stockpiles and foodstuff
[← ↑ → ↓ hyperactive commerce]
 concluding with exam—
in every obsolete Nation

stippled unity

SAFFRON TRAIN

Solemn being
 (on
the left)
subscribes to a minor line---

clambering throng
 (on
the right)
paints the merry town red--------------------- -- - -

Every flight of stairs
ends with a jump—
   (-is-/) triumph indicating,
(-or-is-/) failure ensuing

            ? go back down

Silver-lined clouds
in a
graffitied sky
with Figurines of obscene delight;
no helpmates showing up |···|
God must not be listening today
To the whining
of crying souls,
Backs bleeding
from the labours of a hard day

and rueful sunset

Whilst the melancholy
of tomorrow
yields unremittingly
to the spasms of
Night-life—
aye!*(*^%E@*x----never heard such lunar uttering)

Whispers of peace
dustings of calm;
 spices
and sweet nuts
lift the yellow-orange veil

Now
take off the face—
Step through the door
of my other culture

Regards to my own kind.

THE SETTLEMENT

Certified citizens
are allotting
pine-cones,
posing (one by one)
as a preservationist

_ . [_tumbledown- -] .. . ..

persnickety undergrowth
encircles the fatherland,
in quest of exacting sidelines

Flora is wriggling
through lattice, like
worms escaped from a compost

[social penumbra of the honky]
a moderately shaded
viewpoint
accepts bone-white accolade,
Forgiveness—
there's no such thing

(to which Twin am I speaking) ??

Spider,
drops her silky-smooth trail
onto nearby leaf,

relaying fresh nutrient,

Retrench the soggy
partner
garden-bed too wet
& wishy-washy;
Damsel pansies
in
grubby distress

disgruntled, by
clogged irrigation

refilled my watering can
 With a blonde rainbow.

ENDING SONG

I tried to complete
the surface
of ignorance,
not
the depth of it

high notes
tall tunes
a shrieking placard

Fluid ear
and amplified eyeball
speak an eloquent tongue ~

pessimism
 expunges,
once the realms
of contemporary musician
have resolved
the discordant Sonata of past

clef
double clef;
treble and bass
Expanding the latitudes of
human sound;

the aural canal

of an arcane spirit resonates
with esoteric consolation
(But still) no silent relief
The warriors of competition
go on thrashing their prehistoric drum

Dionysian
finale is
culminating; Remarkably,
one man appears unperturbed
below the rostrum,
lowly platform
suits him benevolently—
He is mitigating the
screeches of mechanisation

bristly patience flew off with the gypsies.

THE ARTIST THAT DID MAUVE

Shy colours
and violet-red streaks,

on a canvas of scratchy
Pain-t
and surface tension

Amalgamated
colour schemes—mixed
 to a
distinctive tint, with
sated brushstrokes and
Resplendent finish;

Skimpy coverings
b l e d to desired consistency
and appropriated textures

Society required an art book
to define
what had no description
other than boorish enmity

Synonymous artworks
led whimsy astray, subjects
colluding with a multitude
of forces; neutral fusions
and settings

free of customary backdrop

Love is encouraged
on a full-time basis
God's credit
is scarlet exhibit
and blue-violet regard

tri-colour and gold,
bright union
of an everlasting stencil.

Acknowledgements:

Some of the poems appearing in this book have been previously published,
either in print or digital format. |

The author wishes to thus acknowledge the editors
and publishers of the following literary journals: |

Poets Union Anthology 2008 (Australia),
Cordite Poetry Review (online) and
Windmills (Deakin University). |

Poems published prior to their appearance in
The Sea In-Between are:
Moving Statue,
Guardian,
Ova,
Snowmaker and
Patriot Lover. |

About the author:

Dianne Cikusa was born in Australia. She grew up in Sydney's south, where she attended high school. |

In 1994, Dianne graduated from the University of Wollongong with a Bachelor of Commerce (Marketing specialisation) and later completed there a Graduate Diploma in Arts (Modern Languages). |

She also holds a Diploma in Language Studies (with French major) from the University of Sydney. |

With an ongoing interest in languages, linguistics and translation, Dianne has since collaborated with various academics and native speakers on the production of a bilingual poetry project. |

About this book:

As we follow the poet's meanderings through verbal stimuli and imagistic prompts, life converges with art and imagination in a vibrant kaleidoscope of visual and perceptual energies, illustrative of the somewhat manic intensity in which we can live our modern lives. The author depicts micro-pictures of a world where small-scale or miscellaneous events remain part of a greater global vision and macrocosmic awareness. It is within this labyrinth of collective memory and personal recollection where we will each replicate the universal human experience. |

In the poet's typical style, a surrealistic mode of expression leads the reader into subconscious terrain, breaking with the ordinariness of the everyday world and the banality of our human routine. There is plenty of symbolism, allusion and wordplay, with the author frequently blurring the lines between "real" and perceived structures as our human energies oscillate between the tangible and the ethereal. Our personal susceptibilities are mirrored by the deconstruction of our thought processes and the malleability of emotion. Like the poems, we may find ourselves at once disjointed and coherent, solving an existing puzzle whilst simultaneously interlocking the pieces of a different one. |

For more information about publications
and other literary developments, visit:

www.mignonpress.com

www.ingramcontent.com/pod-product-compliance
Lightning Source LLC
Chambersburg PA
CBHW070732020526
44118CB00035B/1192